LUCKY 7

SEVEN KEY FUNDAMENTALS FOR LIFE AND SALES

CEL JONAS MARTINEZ

J. JOSEPH GROUP

ISBN 13: 978-0-9979314-4-0

Printed in the USA

J. JOSEPH GROUP

J. Joseph Group, LLC

DISCLAIMER

While the author has taken the utmost effort to ensure the accuracy of the written content, readers are advised to follow the information contained herein at their own risk. The author cannot be held responsible for any personal or commercial damage caused by misinterpretation of information. All readers are encouraged to seek professional advice when needed.

This publication has been written for informational purposes only. Every effort has been made to ensure that it is as complete and accurate as possible. However, there may be mistakes in typography or content. Also, this publication provides information believed to be accurate only up until the date of publication. Therefore, this eBook should be used as a guide, not as an ultimate source.

The purpose of this publication is to educate. The author and the publisher do not warrant that the information contained in this publication is fully complete and shall not be responsible for any errors or omissions. The author and publisher shall have neither liability not responsibility to any person or entity with respect to any loss or damage caused or alleged to be caused directly or indirectly by this publication.

Dedicated to my wife and kids. You have always been a huge part of why I continue to push myself every single day! I'm away for work a lot, and quality family time can be tough to make. I'm blessed that you understand my purpose and have my back 100%. At the end of the journey through ups and downs, God and family is everything, and everything will be okay in the end.

"Here's to the crazy ones.
The misfits. The rebels. The troublemakers.
The round pegs in the square holes.
The ones who see things differently.

They're not fond of rules and they
have no respect for the status quo.
You can quote them, disagree with them,
glorify or vilify them.
About the only thing you can't do is ignore them.

Because they change things.
They push the human race forward.
And while some may see them as the crazy ones,
we see genius.

Because the people who are crazy enough
to think they can change the world,
are the ones who do."

—Steve Jobs

CONTENTS

1

INTRODUCTION

There is a saying attributed to Paulo Coelho: "When you want something with all your heart, the entire universe conspires in helping you achieve it."

This does happen, but only when you are truly ready for it.

I grew up in the small town of El Paso, Texas, born to a single mother. My childhood (along with my two brothers) was nowhere near full of sunshine and smiles. I remember watching my mother rush to work in the early hours of the day and then return home, exhausted from another long day at work. Even while at work, she would wonder about us at home, for we were too young to be left alone. She had no choice but to prioritize work over her kids, for love, care and concern never fed the hunger. While that may sound harsh, her approach and intent was, in actuality, prioritizing her kids over everything.

The nuances of our struggles continued as we grew. I realized that not everyone lived the same type of life we were living. Mowing lawns with my small hands to earn those few bucks to buy the small necessities, I realized how poor we were and how hard it was to make ends meet.

Deep down in my heart, however, I also knew that while we didn't have the high-priced luxuries and the best life has to offer, there were yet others who still had it much worse than we did. Not everyone is born ancestor to a king, but everyone has the innate power and strength to become the king, the ruler of his or her own life and destiny.

Whenever my mind struggled to prioritized what was more necessary to purchase with that small amount of money I earned, I vowed that I would not stay in this place of poverty. I knew that in order to gain prosperity and riches in life, the kind that would no longer cause me to wince at price tags, I had to simply do it, get started, be quick and go the extra mile. I always knew that struggle was a part of life. I knew that prosperity and greatness kiss the feet of those who strive, accept the curveballs life throws at them, embrace their reality and go the extra mile to pursue their dreams.

Nevertheless, it never comes easily. There is no easy path to success. You must climb mountains, carve your own roads and identify the little milestones by which you will measure your journey. Even then, the journey will likely be marred with failures, disappointment and despair, often leading you astray midway through the flight. It will require the courage of a lion combined with the will of a turtle determined with patients to win the race, no matter how slowly you travel or how impossible your circumstances may, at times, seen.

My life has been one such journey from poverty to prosperity. From living in the many rental homes in El

Paso, Texas, to landing in a home I can call my own in a posh town, my life has been a rough expedition of highs and lows as it has been for many others. What truly set me apart, from the rest of the struggling crowd was that I did not surrender in the name of difficulties or blame my circumstances for my despair. Whenever life knocked me cold, choking me until my face turned blue, the light flickering inside of me always made me spring back up on my feet.

There's no shop that sells dreams of passions. Dreams and passions are born from the deep labyrinths of the mind that make one's soul burn with the desire to achieve. It is within those deep labyrinths of our mind that dreams are born and also where fears are created.

> *"Whether you think you can or think you can't, you're right."*

—Henry Ford

I learned that, in the sales industry, decision making and success lie in your own hands. You only have to decide what you want, and in the instant that you do, you are blessed with the power to achieve it. Rejection, distractions and failures are all part of the road to success. During the initial course of my career in the car business, dejecting statements such as, "No, I'm not ready to make my decision," "No, let me think about it," "No, I'm not sure if this is the right vehicle," "No, the price is too high," and "No, let's see another one" certainly dispirited my struggling self at times.

The word "No" would be an important hurdle for me to overcome.

And now, having finished 38 year-long chapters of my book of life, sitting on a comfy chair, in a library located in a serene corner of my 3500-square-foot home, here I am, sharing the story of my not-so-fairytale life. I started from the bottom and eventually made it this far, so far. I didn't surrender to the unfavorable circumstances from which my life started. I chose what I wanted to do with the hands I was dealt along the way instead of settling for them. I hope that my story will serve as inspiration for all of the enthusiasts who have been stuck in the spiral of life's unpleasant surprises, but have kept their heart warm by the flickering flame of desire that fuels them to keep going and progressing until they land on what they aimed for.

This book is intended to be pure inspiration, not a mere bundle of stacked-up pages, with cleverly jotted-down words. It is an open-for-all treasure of some of my real-life experiences. What I've learned throughout the journey and what I learned from several great books, mentors and gurus I was blessed to come across along the way.

I will share what I've learned about success first-hand as well as the key fundamentals that accelerated my journey to success. I've had people tell me that I'm lucky to be where I am today, but I disagree. I believe my success is because of seven fundamentals that have helped me through my journey. The reason I titled this book *Lucky 7* is because, in my life, those seven key fundamentals have continuously pulled me forward along my life journey.

I believe that success is preceded by divine signs or, as you have probably heard, success leaves clues. Who knows, this book could end up being your shooting star, or the destiny's call, for you to get on your mark and set off headstrong onto the journey in pursuit of happiness, success and prosperity.

2

ATTITUDE

"The greatest discovery of my generation is that man can after his life simply by altering his attitude of mind."

—James Truslow Adams

If you find yourself stuck in a place where, despite having all the talent, all the skills and all the abilities in the world, you simply cannot seem to move forward, let me tell you what possibly could be holding you back: YOUR ATTITUDE.

My experiences have taught me that simply having the skills to do something is only a part of the deal; your attitude is just as important. In fact, in looking back, it is safe to say that, were it not for my attitude I likely would have had lost the battle before it even started.

Keeping your head above water and forever retaining the hope for a better tomorrow in your heart are by no means easy tasks, especially if you work in the sales arena, where you frequently hear the word "No."

Rejection can be lethal, but only if you let it. Everyone has his own share of problems his own experience with doors being slammed in his face and his own disappointing moments where in a customer passed in search of something better. The rejection isn't what matters; what matters is what you do with that rejection.

Of course, what you choose to do with the curveballs that life pitches in your direction is your right but internalizing the negativity that comes in the form of rejections, failures and disappointments spread it like a cancer through your system. Once you start thinking along the lines that you cannot do something, you truly will not be able to do it unless you begin thinking otherwise.

The psychology behind this is actually pretty simple. Consider yourself someone who has not been able to strike a car sale for the past five days, for whatever reason. Five days of not having things going your way can be frustrating. Believe me, I know. All the angst inside you builds and builds and every new customer you meet, an inner voice in your head asks, what makes you think this time is going to be any different than the other experiences you have had for the past five days? Vulnerable, you give into that voice and automatically lose all the spark, all the motivation to try harder. You become disinterested in walking someone new through the process because you have accepted defeat before the battle began. You no longer want to persuade someone because you think to yourself, "What is the use of these futile attempts?"

These futile attempts are exactly what may lead you to your success. One of my mentors taught me what it truly means to stand up seven times when you have been knocked down six times. He taught me that when life is really pushing you and really testing your limits, you always have a choice of how you respond to it. The seven different directions in which you are being pulled right now could be bending you to better position you or they could be destroying you; it is all about having the right attitude towards your circumstances. Remember, you always have a choice.

"My attitude is that if you push me towards something that you think is a weakness, then I will turn that perceived weakness into a strength."

—Michael Jordan

Since learning this lesson, each time I've been met with a "No," I've come up with a "Yes" of my own. I did this and still do this through one simple method: looking at the bright side. With so much negativity surrounding us, it can be difficult to maintain a positive attitude toward life in general as well as your particular struggles, but this is when the true growth occurs. What does not challenge you will not change you; it's as simple as that.

If you survey all of the influential people you have encountered in your life, you will soon likely notice that most of them have one thing in common: they have the right attitude and mindset. I, myself, am a living example of how the right mindset and attitude can get you pretty far in life. I choose not to be defined by my failures; I choose to be inspired by them. This is how I got where I am today.

Of course, this is easier said than done. As someone who used to be very optimistic but became someone who lost faith in his own self, not to mention the world around him, and then returned to a place of finding and loving myself, I understand just how much power each of us has inside of ourselves. In retrospect, I can easily say that, were it not for the more bitter of challenging experiences in my life, I probably would never have been able to discover my true strength. There is a saying that you never really know how strong you are until being strong is the only option you have.

In many ways, I grew tired of my own negativity. I was naturally high on life, so it makes sense that I didn't respond well to the toll the negativity was taking on me. You might wonder why I let my negativity take its toll on me in the first place and Truth be told, it is a bit hard to be positive when the people around you seem to be on some sort of lifelong mission to misunderstand you. It is even harder to be positive when you have only a $20 bill in your pocket with an entire month stretched in front of you.

Notice that while I say the word "hard," never have I said the word "impossible." Harsh and tougher realities often have a way of seeping in your life, right into you, through your skin, without you even noticing. I really do not know exactly when I went form a happy-go-lucky child to someone who had toxicity flowing through his blood, but what I did know was that I did not get there on my own. The bitter people in my life were one of the main reasons I had started to lose faith in myself and my abilities. Therefore, I decided that, before doing anything else, I needed to change the company I surrounded myself with.

Let me do the honor of reminding you that attitudes are contagious. I came across such amazing people in my life who just as I did, started from scratch and ended up running empires. Their spirit and attitude were contagious, and I made sure that I caught them.

My mentors, including my twin brother (iron sharpens iron), had a huge impact in my life. They taught me that it does not matter what happens to you in life, what matters is what happens in your mind when something happens in your life. I was taught that if I did not let go of the "I can't do it" attitude, it would take root and the roots would run so deep inside of who I am as a person that the negativity would become a part of my character, a part of my subconscious.

I decided to put my foot down and grab hold of the adverse circumstances rather than allow the adverse circumstances to get a hold of me. I asked myself what I wanted most, and my immediate answer was: "excellence." The next thing I told myself was that if excellence is what I was striving for, I needed to start developing the habits and the mindset to match. You can only correct something when you know what it is that needs to be corrected. Not only did I begin to keenly observe what others were saying or doing to me that were making me think of myself as less of a person, I also started taking notes on how I was responding to my own self. I asked myself when this thought first hit me, and it saddened me quite a bit. You never truly need anyone as much as you need your own self. In fact, I'm confident that this belief alone can be transformational. It should be included in everyone's survival of the fittest kit: you never need anyone as much as you need your own self. After all is said and done, you go to bed with the person you are. You need to be your own best friend.

Do not get me wrong, I am not encouraging people to abandon their relationships and live the life of a hermit. Human relationships are important in a person's life, but it's not healthy depending on someone else for your happiness and success. If you want to succeed, you want your happiness, and nobody on this entire planet will want it as badly as you do. Hence, the effort that you put forth will have to be like no other.

If you find yourself stuck in a situation where nothing seems to be working, laugh about it, sometimes you have to let go with a little laugh and remember that there are controllable and uncontrollable facets of life.

Your attitude is controllable. Never ever give up, no matter where you are. Stay humble and keep moving forward. Try to take those first few steps—the ones that always seem to be the hardest after having your limbs badly bruised and battered. I promise, you will not regret it.

Life is going to challenge you every now and then. Remember, that is a part of the process; that is what most people don't want to go through. Everybody wants to be a millionaire, but they don't want to go through the process required to become one. If I start telling myself that I have made it and it is now, therefore, okay to start compromising on my principles and hard work, believe me it would not be long before I fell back into the pit I crawled out of. Don't get me wrong, affirmations are great. In fact, it's okay to talk to yourself with positive affirmations, spend time with yourself and spend time on yourself. Spend time with people who bring out the best in you. However, what I'm also saying is, don't have the mindset as if you already arrived, believe me there is always more to accomplish.

This is the thing about life: it will not stop testing you. If you're moving forward with the right attitude, learning is easier as you go on with new experiences and new challenges. You must have patience and resilience while at it. You have to have the right attitude. Not to sound cliché, but you can learn something every day. I've found that a great attitude is one of the most important things to have to succeed in life and sales.

3

STUDENT MENTALITY

"The capacity to learn is a gift; the ability to learn is a skill but the willingness to learn is a matter of your choice"

—Brian Hervert

An expert in anything was born a beginner.
He must have conceived some ideas in his brain.

The ideas must have kept him awake through those long, sleepless nights, planning and seeking out ways to turn them into a reality. He consistently wondered how to best pursue his goal.

He likely failed mightily in his initial attempts. He was likely rejected suffered from hopelessness and perhaps even came to the verge of giving up altogether.

But he persisted.

And instead of giving up, he learned!

He learned from his mistakes, and he improved upon his techniques through his learning as well as the wisdom he gained through his failures.

He simply tried over and over again.

And then, slowly, as a caterpillar turns into a butterfly, he transformed into an expert, a maestro, an ultimate champion.

He, who was only once a beginner!

This is the generic blueprint of the story of all champions and achievers. Nobody is born a champion. Champions are made. It's more accurate to say that champions are self-made because the only person that is going to make it happen is you. No one else is going to do it for you. You may have help along the way, of course, by surrounding yourself with the right people. Champions turn their can'ts into cans and their dreams into plans. They equip themselves with the right tools. They learn the rules of the game and they learn them so well that they know how to change them, mold them and use them to their advantage. It is this thirst for learning that fuels them to keep up with their plans. It is through their passion to know more and more that they excel and grow. Learning is an ongoing process from cradle to grave. It is the desire to learn more that develops a student mentality, and student mentality is another essential ingredient, another key fundamental for success and prosperity.

I believe that if you identify one thing that can almost surely lead you to success, it's the willingness to have a student mentality. Having a student mentality allows for acceptance of the fact that you are not a know-it-all. And, when you realize that you know nothing in its absolute entirety, the flame of curiosity sparks in your soul and ignites into your passion. It is your student mentality that leverages your self-confidence and belief that if you can learn anything, you can do or become anything. This is a universal phenomenon. When you learn something, you get better at it. The more you learn, the better you get. The better you get, the more you succeed. Learning, implementation, improvement and success are the components of a cyclic process. It goes on and never stops, and this is why it is said that success has no limits.

Learning does not necessarily have to be confined to a classroom with a teacher. However, the great thing about it is that you can simultaneously be the student and the teacher. You can learn through your mistakes. You can learn through other people's successes and mistakes. You can learn through observation or through audio or videos. If you are willing to learn, there are many resources that can be your teacher. When I was struggling to get on my feet, make a career and excel in life, there were a number of things that could have let me down and they did try to bring me down but I kept my mind open to learning and getting better and sharper.

I was a salesman, selling door-to-door. Direct selling tests your strengths. Doors are slammed shut in your face and you have to keep your attitude under control while it's happening. You must get used to a lot of rejections. As a door-to-door salesman, I learned the basic tenets of various sales techniques.

I kept my mind working and my eyes open. I learned from people involved in a similar profession. I observed how they did their job and it wasn't only about the winners. I also kept an eye on those who were not doing well. That is how I learned which skills I needed to excel and which I should avoid. It was through this observation that I learned how to present myself, how to make an offer, how to maintain eye contact, how to retain energy and enthusiasm, and how to overcome objections.

I remember a time in life when I would look at people and things longingly and wonder, *How can people survive with so little and yet achieve so much in their life?* They have spacious homes, luxurious cars and all the pricey bounties life has to offer. I was young, about 22 years old, and recently engaged. I once took my wife (then my fiancé) to a sales meeting with a prospect, held at his palatial apartment. His home had everything one could wish for. Everything spoke for its worth and value, and the owner of it all--my sales prospect himself--appeared well off and clean cut. He exuded the aura of wealth.

The meeting went well, or at least as well as any sales meeting could go. However, a thought was constantly stroking the back of my mind throughout our time together.

I wondered, "While this guy has accomplished many things that I haven't? What does he have that I don't?" During the entire conversation, half of my mind was focused on the sales and leasing processes we were discussing, while the other half was constantly reminding me, "If he can do it, what's your excuse?" I do not mean to say that I was considering myself as being perfect or the best or better in any way. Rather, I felt a reassurance that I could be better myself, that I could excel and that I could accomplish everything that I hadn't yet.

I shared my thoughts with my fiancée, and she reassured me that if I thought it, it must be both true and doable. It was at that moment that I decided not to spend my life selling door-to-door. I realized I must broaden my learning horizon by venturing into something new, for then I could get closer to my dreams and everything else I wished to achieve.

Having made up my mind to make a career change, I inhaled hope and took a leap of faith. I received a call for an interview by the district manager at The Crossing, a pretty nice apartment leasing business in Las Vegas. I was confident. Just as they do in all job interviews, the district manager asked me why they should hire me. After all, I did not have any experience in apartment leasing. My response: "Because you need a closer, a go-getter in that role. You said you need to have a 95% occupancy of your units. I'm the guy you need because I close deals and will keep great relationships to sustain occupancy."

I was hired.

Sales itself was not new for me, but leasing apartments was. Nevertheless, I had this faith, this great attitude that I could learn and become excellent. As a result of my confidence, my enthusiasm, the fuel of my dreams and my penchant for learning and growth, I excelled at my new career. I learned the basics and became a pro. I continued to learn and grow, so much so that I became the top salesman in the district and was eventually promoted to a manager.

Looking back, I realized that it was my student mentality that pushed me forward to new levels. Of course, the job itself was never a piece of cake, but I had a learning attitude. I have seen many people fail, merely because they think they know it all and cannot be taught anymore. They believe that they have enough innate skills to ace the job. This is sometimes the roadblock to improvement and learning that causes people to lag in the race of life.

I still consider myself a student. I still feel that I have the capacity to learn more, and it is this drive that compels me to seek learning and improvement every single day. Whether my brother, my mentors, a good read or anything else that sparks up a learning curiosity, I leave behind no opportunity to better myself and learn something new. I strongly believe that this is an essential key to growth on the path to prosperity.

I believe that life itself is quite similar to sales. Your entire life is a process of buying and selling. Sometimes the selling is abstract, as in an idea, a thought or a feeling that you share. Other times, you aim to sell something tangible such as a toy you wanted when you were young. You tried to sell your wish to your parents, to convince them to buy it for you. When you grow up, you must negotiate on matters of both minor and dire importance with your spouse, with your peers and with your prospects.

Almost every aspect of life comes down to buying and selling and not only in terms of money. You must keep track of your actions and reactions. You must be willing to both know and learn if you wish to excel. At the same time, you must accept that learning can obviously be beneficial if it's specific or directed to what your pursuing such as a vision or goals or targeted to determined accomplishments. You will come across a variety of lessons that you might believe will come in handy at some time in your life. You will be distracted and detoured by lessons you mistake as useful. Do not, I repeat, do not get involved in just anything and everything. You cannot possibly head in four directions at once. Therefore, you may as well be selective about what is it that you want to excel at and where it is that you wish to land in life. When you specifically envision what you want to be and where you wish to stand, it will be far clearer which path and knowledge will take you there.

The good news is that learning and student mentality don't have to be inborn traits; they can be learned. If you have a burning desire and a passion to grow, excel and succeed, congratulations! You have cleared the first stage. A desire to grow and an acceptance of one's capacity to learn more are the prime roots of excellence. I'm not speaking only to my personal philosophy with regard to my profession, I'm also speaking to the sales job itself. If you are, or want to be a, doctor, lawyer, pilot or astronaut, you must learn the intricacies of that specific industry. You have the power to choose your playing field and you must learn the rules of it. You must arm yourself with a shield of knowledge in order to protect yourself from badly hurting yourself when you trip and fall. Every profession is a game, a marathon of sorts and the only way to win is to never stay content with what you know at any given point in time.

As does every other living thing, thoughts, ideas and learnings decay over time. You must stay fresh through a consistent input of more knowledge, wisdom, intellect and information. You must ensure that the soil within your brain is consistently fed with the fodder it needs since this is the place from which success and prosperity will cultivate. A mentor, an inspiration and/or a role model will sure keep you on the right track, but in the end, no one but you has the power to decide if you will stop or continue to grow.

Knowledge is power. You know that. But what good is power that is not exercised? Suppose you stood facing the border of a battlefield, armed with all the shields and weapons available to you, knowing that the ensuing battle is a matter of life and death. Imagine deciding not to use your tools but instead to leaving the end result up to fate. If you closed your eyes to all that was ahead thinking you would survive, would you?

Of course not. You would be doomed. You would be stomped on and thrown out of the battlefield. You would lose.

This is what happens in your professional life as well. When you have the knowledge and the skills, when you know that you can learn and excel by having a student mentality, what 's your excuse if you're not doing it?

Do you want to carry a load of regrets that will torment you in your old age, when your limbs will shake and your eyes will be blind? Do you want these regrets to continue to pierce the pieces of your soul, reminding you how different life would have been had you only taken that leap of faith? Knowing I don't want to ever find myself saying, "If only…." I consistently encouraged myself to hone my skills and the power I had having that student mentality. No pain is more excruciating than the pain of regret.

There are two ways you can lead your life: like the billions of others who came and went without actually doing anything significant, or like those few who dared to challenge their circumstances, pursued learning, had that student mentality, aspired to their dreams and never settled on their present.

First, they discovered what they wanted out of life. Then they learned how to achieve their goals. Finally, they learned how to excel. This chain reaction triggered their growth and progression and brought them a stature few in the world have achieved.

In the words of Aristotle:

"Excellence is an art won by training and habituation. We do not act rightly because we have virtue or excellence, but we rather have those because we have acted rightly. We are what we repeatedly do. Excellence, then, is not an act but a habit."

4

CONFIDENCE

"If you have no confidence in self, you are twice defeated in the race of life. With confidence you have won even before you have started."

—Marcus Garvey

Buddha once said, "What you think, you become. What you feel, you attract and what you imagine you create."

I would add to that, what you are repeatedly told, you eventually believe!

When your mind is consistently fed certain information, hard as you may try to resist it, it begins to form roots in your mind and you unconsciously start to believe it. I would not have believed that could happen had I not been through that exact experience during the younger years of my life.

I am a born extrovert. I was a happy-go-lucky child, with a free soul and a penchant for socializing even at a young age despite the unfavorable circumstances in which I grew up. I opened my eyes by knowing it could always be worse; I was too high on life to be let down by adversity.

I started talking a bit earlier and a lot more than does a typical child. I had so much going on inside my mind that I wanted to express and share with not just my mother or brothers but anyone present who paid even the slightest bit of attention or showed the smallest amount of interest in what I had to say. I was fond in getting in touch with people, and I loved to make friends regardless of others age. In fact, my brother and I thought that all older people were our grandma and grandpa. We even called them grandma and grandpa.

Maybe because they were more open and attentive, listening to my nonstop chattering more than young folks and I loved the way they would smile, and their eyes would glisten with joy when I talked to them about anything, but I could talk for hours and hours on any topic even without a specific topic to start the discussion with older people.

While this could have been seen as a sign of being a unique child with a bit more intelligence than a typical kid of the same age, it was unfortunately perceived the opposite way. I began to be labeled a "motor mouth," and it was none other than my mother, grandma and aunt who would tell me to shut up and that I talked too much.

"Celvadore, you talk too much. You are just a motor mouth."

"You talk too much for your age. Kids don't talk that much. Go and play."

"You are too loud."

"Why are you so noisy?"

This is what my mother, grandmother and aunt consistently said. Every time I wanted to share a new story or something I saw during the day or anything else that I wanted to talk about, I was interrupted mid-way by one of these statements. It was even more discouraging because such response was coming not from strangers but from my own blood relatives, my elders, the people I believed I could count on. That made it hurt even more. We grow from infant to child with a belief that our family, our support system, will stand by our side when someone else says something negative like this to us. Unfortunately, I was too young to know that the issue didn't lie with me. At times, I wondered if my family even loved me in the first place.

They did love me, but they just didn't hear me at times. My young mind was too small to understand why and, eventually, I turned silent. An invisible cocoon began to form around me, enclosing my vibrant personality within self-established boundaries. I began to devalue myself, assuming I was noisy, annoying and less loved by my family. This cast a sharp blow to my innate confidence, and over time, I stopped being the child who was high on energy and instead more on eggshells about saying or doing anything.

The major effect of being called a motor mouth along with my relatives' seemingly simple requests for me to shut up was most notably observed when I was around nine years old and had to perform in "Pompeii," a school play. Despite all the pre-play work and rehearsals we went through, on the day when I had to perform in front of the crowd, I froze on stage. The child who once would not stay silent for even a minute was speechless. I had forgotten the script, and words seemed to find no way out of my mouth.

"You are a motor mouth." "You are too loud." "Shut up and go play outside." These statements began echoing in my mind and constraining my will to be normal, and cheerful self. Once the play was over I walked off feeling as though I failed.

That is how it works. The human mind is a strange place. Even your God-gifted talents do not work for you if they are not nurtured, and you may fail even if you have all the requisite capabilities mastered. If you have that dark corner in your mind that consistently reminds you that you cannot do it, that you are not capable, you will eventually believe it and won't be able to do it anymore.

As I mentioned before, the final outcome is determined by your state of mind. "Whether you think you can or think you can't, you're right." Remember, by definition, belief is the acceptance that a statement is true or that some-thing does exist, and confidence is the right-hand of belief. If you believe in something, you will be able to confidently execute it.

Belief is confidence and confidence is belief. In my case, my innate abilities started to become over-shadowed by those dejecting directives I consistently received. Words and experiences, no matter how insignificant they might seem in a moment have a huge potential and they have a permanent impact on your mind. They root themselves deep down in your sub-conscious, and you do not even realize that desolate corner of your mind is breeding fears that will only grow and flourish and hold you back anytime you are supposed to do something great or out of routine.

You will find yourself believing that you do not have it in you to make it to the other side of fear, that your cocoon is a safe place and that you should not break free of its limitations, that a world of endless possibilities is nothing but an illusion, that the real world is hard but you should compromise and settle for it since you do not have the courage to change for good. With this magnitude of negativity bubbling inside and taking control of your strengths and optimism, how do you stay confident and restore positive self-belief?

Every action has its equal and opposite reaction. Newton's law applies equally when it comes to human psychology. If your mind can produce fears, it has an equal capacity to counter and overcome those fears. When your mind senses an obstacle, it also has the ability to find a way out. In order to do this, you need to identify the sub-conscious belief that is nurturing your mind and feeding your demons. You must identify it and accept it in its entirety, for only then will you be able to overcome and go through it. You must realize that life happens outside your comfort zone; only you can break through those barriers that exist in your mind. And remember, knowing is part of overcoming those fears and being confident.

If you are able to come across a mentor or coach who can become your beacon of inspiration and guide you through the journey, or if you are surrounded by determined, strong willed go-getters you will unconsciously develop a similar winning faith and belief. That is why it is important to spend time with optimistic, positive people (winners). When you let go of things holding you back and prepare to embrace what is coming next, you will eventually develop a confidence that will raise your set of self-beliefs.

I was fortunate enough to have my twin brother on my side as an extra support system as well as an extra push of motivation. I was also fortunate to have my wife, along with mentors who did not accuse or blame me or ever make me feel or think poorly of myself. I had mentors who became my inspiration not only through their words but also through their deeds or actions. They made me realize that I had a similar set of strengths and capacities to become like them or even better.

As I said earlier, what you are consistently told you eventually believe; just as I had once believed I was not capable of much, I began to realize that I was wrong. I was worthy of anything that I could achieve. If it was meant to be, it was up to me.

A mentor, counselor or coach can only guide you and motivate you to set out on your journey and help pursue your goals, however. The most important key to unlocking your personal barriers lies in your own hands. In the end, no one else can unlock that door for you. You are the creator of your own destiny and only you have the power to make it happen.

Public speaking was an extreme fear of mine. As a matter of fact, public speaking is one of the top five things people most fear. To add insult to injury, I was promoted to a sales manager position driven by speaking to both small and large crowds. Avoiding interaction with people only meant that I would fail big time. I realized that in order to survive and excel, I needed to get rid of this weakness. I looked up some great mentors each and every time I had a chance. I saw and observed how they addressed others in public and how they kept potentially profitable conversation going. I also realized that even they would sometimes come across a difficult or unpleasant situation; nonetheless, they still handled it well and turned it to their advantage.

This observation and learning (practice) that I gained through meeting with people and mentors made me realize that I can speak publicly and that I can address crowds and reach out to the masses. It was as convenient for me as it was for my mentors. With this realization, I was able to get to the core of my issue, the root cause behind why I was lagging behind and the barriers that were preventing me from moving forward.

It is often said that comparing yourself to others is actually devaluing yourself in your own eyes. I disagree with that.

I think that if you compare yourself with the ones you look up to or the ones who inspire you, you will eventually catch their positive attributes and start developing a similar competitive attitude. You will subconsciously adopt some of their key habits. This only works, however, if you have a will and the optimism to focus on the positives. With an icon of success and inspiration to look toward, you are much more likely to believe that you, too, can do it.

It invokes a feeling of certainty in you, ensuring that your vision is realistic and achievable. This feeling of being certain, being sure, being true to self, combined with strong belief in one's self is the ultimate definition of confidence. It's the self-belief that fuels your will and determination and triggers your action.

You need to realize your worth, evaluate your strengths and get past your weaknesses. This is how you develop self-assurance, a self-acknowledgement of your skills and abilities and breaking through to the place in which you are comfortable.

When you do not know what is holding you back or what you are afraid of, you will not be able to get past it. When you know what is blocking your way, you know how to push it aside and pave your way forward. As the Bible says, "And you shall know the truth and the truth shall set you free." Accepting your innermost truths, your deepest fears, your darkest demons and your ultimate reality will set you free. When you let go of your fears you can embrace better and constructive emotions that will act as catalysts in pursuit of your goals. Anytime I do something new that frightens or challenges me, I feel a fresh surge of energy and a brisk effervescence of joy and excitement running in my bones.

Anything that makes your adrenaline rush or ignites a winning spark is worth doing. All you need is belief and faith in your heart that when your mind can think it, it certainly has the power to achieve it. Ideas are the abstract brainchild of the mind and it is your mind, your perception of self and your faith and belief that decide if those ideas can turn into concrete reality. Having confidence in oneself is key to continuing to press forward in the journey of life and all of one's endeavors.

It clarifies that you have the potential to do better, and it means that you are capable of performing even better than you presently are. When you have a learning mentality and a penchant for excellence, it ignites a spark that keeps you restless, motivates you to strive and never lets you settle for less than what you are able to achieve. In the words of Nelson Mandela, "There is no passion to be found in playing small, in settling for a life that is less than the one you are capable of living."

5

WORK ETHIC

*"The difference between a successful person and others is not
a lack of strength, not a lack of knowledge,
but rather, a lack of will."*

A lack in your will indicates a lack in your core work ethic.

Kathy Ireland once said, "Keep integrity and your work ethic intact. So what if that means working a little harder; an honorable character is your best calling card and that's something anyone can have!"

Work ethic is something anyone can have, but not many people have it. The reason people do not have it is, they do not understand why it's beneficial, how it actually works, and how it propels them on their path to prosperity.

Because not everyone has work ethic, not everyone is a champion. I'm certainly not saying that you only have to work hard; work ethic is only one piece of the puzzle. Having a great work ethic also means that you work smart. Those with strong and unwavering work ethic are ultimate champions, the go-getters. No matter how long their journey, they will eventually win against all odds.

With that said, it should be clear exactly what work ethic constitutes. But how does one distinguish between the winning and the chanting crowd?

By popular definition, work ethic is a set of elements that forms the basis of the philosophy that hard work is intrinsically virtuous or worthy of reward. The mantra of work ethic revolves around the founding core of hard work, and I believe that to be true. Personally, I would not restrict the idea of work ethic merely to a definition, thereby limiting its scope. I prefer to divide the concept of work ethic into two distinct parts: work and ethic.

If we begin with the dictionary of work, it is and action, an activity or a series of actions that involves a mental or physical effort with predetermined purpose, goals or objective. Therefore, hard work infers that you are putting in your optimal mental and physical efforts. People often comment that hard work will leave you feeling lethargic, that it will put on you an extra load of stress and that it will not make you rich or successful. It has also been said that smart work is better than hard work, and that working smart is the only way to excel in present-age competition.

I believe that hard work is, in fact, an essential piece to success. Hard work means that you have put forth your best potential as well as your ultimate capabilities. It means that you are using your own thought processes, by developing your own vision and perception, and that you are getting things done in your own way, rather than just relying on conventional processes or following one prevalent practice. It means that you are going the extra mile, putting in additional efforts and working extra hours in pursuit of your purpose and goals.

Parallel to that, ethics in the literal sense of the term is a set of moral codes, your core values, principles and beliefs and your ideas the ideal approach toward something. In a professional context, ethics entails adequate knowledge, ideas and core values surrounding the way that something should be done in the best and most logically justifiable manner. Ethics evolve when you have a deep and sound understanding of the intricacies of a job, and you know what exactly then is the best way to do that job.

Therefore, combining the definitions of work and ethics, we can suggest that, in cumulative sense, your work ethic is your mantra, your credo, and your philosophy based on your knowledge, experience and expertise, to perform the right actions, in the right manner and the right direction toward your specific goals.

In its simplest form, your work ethic is a standard of conduct for job performance. Each job domain, each professional and all operational areas of your career or even your life as a whole has its own unique work ethic, as per their nature of each job and its vision, mission and goals.

In my world, the establishment of concrete work ethic makes a huge difference and is actually probably the most significant and fundamental element of success. The idea of success is not everyone's cup of tea and, apparently not everyone can brew success even if they have the right recipe because they do not want to put in the work. They don't have the required work ethic.

With a more thorough understanding of the concept of work ethic, it will be easier to know and understand the essential factors and core values that make up and influence your own personal work ethic. For me, it's confidence, faith and belief in yourself and your efforts; the attitude and approach you have towards your responsibilities; your student mentality; your acceptance of the fact that you have the potential to learn and improve, and the amount of hard work and solid effort you put into a task that forms the foundation of one's work ethic.

When you have an optimistic and progressive attitude toward your specific goal, it builds up a confidence whereby you believe that if you put in the proper efforts, you will skillfully ace the task. Attitude and confidence go hand-in-hand, and a set vision or goal triggers both in a person. When you know what it is that your pursuing, it becomes easier to choose which specific effort to put in, your confidence builds, positively influencing your attitude.

The key, therefore, to evolving the attitude and belief elements of constructive work ethic is to eliminate the ambiguities and be specific and clear about your goals. It is only at that point when you will know how to lay construct your path and sharpen your skills in order to compel yourself into action with a strong belief that you have the power, you have the guts and you have the potential to succeed. As Arnold Schwarzenegger said, "The secret is contained in a three-part formula I learned in the gym:

self-confidence; a positive mental attitude; and honest, hard work."

The other crucial element of strong work ethic is student mentality. As discussed in the previous chapter, student mentality is the ultimate acceptance of the fact that there is room and space in you that represents, a potential and capability to learn more, improve yourself and move ahead. It has nothing to do with your lack of expertise, your flaws or your incapability. It is a mere indication of the fact that there is always room to become a better version of yourself.

It clarifies that you have the potential to do better, and it means that you are capable of performing even better than you presently are. When you have a learning mentality and a penchant for excellence it ignites a spark that keeps you restless, motivates you to strive and never lets you settle on less than what you are able to achieve. In the words of Nelson Mandela, "There is no passion to be found in playing small, in settling for a life that is less than the one you are capable of living."

Furthermore, hard work is another critical component of well-grounded work ethic. Many people argue that the concept of hard work is now outdated and that smart work is now in vogue. While that may be true in some cases, as I look upon genuine success stories, I find that they have one thing in common: hard work. Success does not come easily. Success has no short cuts. Success does not arrive via a magic wand. It requires efforts, and it demands dedication.

If you are doing the same amount of work as everyone else, you will not be able to get ahead of them. You will maintain the same rank. If you want to excel, be competitive and sprint ahead in the race, you will need to put in your best additional effort. The initial phase of the race is always the crammed and cluttered, with the ordinary. But those who dare to excel bypass the rest and are willing to go the extra mile. There is no traffic jam there because not everyone dares to make it beyond a specific point. You can work hard or you can work smart, but, why not do both?

Remember if you are putting in 100% the person in front of you is putting in 110% and that is why he is ahead of you. You could fall behind at any moment because the person behind you is putting in 120% and aiming for your spot. If you keep up with your sustained efforts, you will lag behind by a great margin. If you want to escalate your rank, you need a consistent dose of additional effort so that you will not only sustain your standing but also progress to pick up the next spot and ultimately get ahead in the race.

Hard work never goes out of style. It's the ultimate fuel to trigger growth. Even if you have certain weaknesses or are lagging behind in certain skills, hard work will compensate for many of the shortcomings, flaws and discrepancies. The potential and scope of hard work is so infinitely broad that you can simply never do enough of it. There will always be room for more. Eventually, hard work implies that the scope of success, too, is infinite. In fact, the harder you work, the luckier you get and the higher you will elevate. The sky will no longer be the limit. Instead, it will serve only as your first destination.

You might wonder how to work harder, how to further increase your efforts. There are times when we all want to give up. There are times that we all think that were finished. There are times that we think we simply cannot do it anymore. Our tolerance and patience are tested and the clouds of despair engulf our motivation. It is that moment when our attitude steps up as our savior. It is our attitude, our optimism and our self-belief that makes us spring back to life in the ring of competition or domination and compel us to fight, to work harder and harder. We do not lose when we are defeated; we lose when we accept defeat.

A positive attitude and an unwavering confidence will never allow us to accept defeat. They serve as a beacon of assurance, a reminder that there is still a chance, that we still have hope. Only if we try, putting in our best with a strong belief in self and a positive approach, will we succeed and achieve whatever it is that we are pursuing.

Your work ethic will not develop and strengthen if you do not fuel it with the right tools. Work ethic develops a byproduct of the acquisition of a set of principles, rules and values that are sustained long-term until they become a habit. You must continue to do things in a certain way until a blueprint is formed and becomes engraved in your genes.

When you have a work ethic blueprint, it becomes easier to align and lay any dream or goal with or over it and you will more quickly and clearly know the areas that need to be fixed and worked on to make your dream turn into a reality.

Joe Frazier once said, "*You can map out a fight plan or a life plan, but when the action starts, it may not go the way you planned and you're down to your reflexes that means your preparation. That's where your roadwork shows. If you cheated on that in the dark of the morning, well, you're going to get found out now, under the bright lights."*

Therefore, even if things go against your initial plan, your strong work ethic will keep you grounded and determined to fight again. On whatever level you have been defeated, your work ethic will always provide a strong and rock-solid ground zero, to make a fresh start, a new beginning, over and over again.

When we talk about work ethic and specifically debate over whether it is that hard work or the smart work that counts more, it helps to understand the concepts of effectiveness and efficiency doing the right things and doing things right. The terms are often confused, yet there exists a strong basic difference between the two.

Being effective means that you know your job, you know what to do and you do it. How you do it, does not matter. Effectiveness is only confined to getting things done by any means necessary. Being efficient, however, is different. Being efficient requires that you get things done the right way keeping your resources, time and efforts under strict control and producing the optimum outputs with just the right input of time and efforts.

Whether through effectiveness or efficiency, things will ultimately get done. But efficiency that is, doing things in the right way, will minimize the required input of resources. It is what allows you to devise and follow the one best way to get the job done. This eventually drives you to complete more, thereby exceling and taking you ahead in the arena.

Always remember that perfection is an illusion; there is only process. You cannot let things wait, you cannot let things stand by and you cannot keep things on hold. The best time to get anything done is right now. If you look for perfection, you will never be content. If you keep on waiting, you will be waiting for the rest of your life. Perfection should never be your end goal, but you can certainly incorporate it into your process and carry it in your mentality as a part of your professional credo. Do not deceive yourself, however, for perfection exists only in utopia, and in reality, it can never be achieved. Perfection should not be your center of gravity. It is simply the effort you put in, the drive and the goals. As said by a previous mentor, "It is the push."

There is a saying that, "Perfection is an illusion, sought by those who fail to understand that our flaws are what motivates us to always be better."

So, whether it's your personal or professional domain of life, remember these three basic rules:

Things are temporary!
Things are imperfect!
Things are incomplete!

You must accept anything for what it truly is, embracing it in its utmost entirety. You do not have to worry pondering over the flaws, shortcomings and discrepancies. Things do not get done on their own. Your goals will not magically fall into your lap. Your wishes, dreams and desires won't turn into reality on their own. You have to get things done. You have to take action. You have to inhale your optimism, trust your wings and dive into that great leap of faith. If you don't and instead continue to wait for the right time and moment, then you will forget that the competition is increasing with every passing moment.

Remember the person behind you is putting in 120% to outclass you and take your position. If you don't act now, the world will walk all over you and you will be crushed in the stampede of competition. Keep your hard work and efficiency aligned, choose the right tasks, the right goals and the right paths and get them done right, the best and the smartest way. This is the simplest description of the way that productivity and work ethic work together.

In even more simple terms, as Tim Ferris said, *"Focus on being productive instead of busy."*

Right from the start, I knew that tasks require planning and planning requires action. If you want to get something, there is no other way to do so. I embraced work ethic as part of my winning tools and lucky seven key fundamentals for success. The first and foremost fundamental of a strong work ethic is punctuality. When you want to get something done, be on time. Punctuality is key to initiating your action in the most beneficial way.

Having a code of conduct is also absolutely essential in executing your plan in pursuit of success. Be on time. Be a little earlier and stay a little longer if you want to do more. Your work, your goals and your success are your responsibility. You cannot sit back, relax and procrastinate and think that you will get things done. There are times I have to work a little longer than I am supposed to, and there are times when I have to show up a bit earlier than others. In times like these do not think that you are being too hard on yourself and that the job is asking too much of you. It is not.

There is a saying that flashes in my mind whenever I am supposed to do something more or when I have to struggle a bit more to get my work done: *"Don't quit when you're tired. Quit when you're done."*

When you have delved into something, when you have put your energy in a startup or a goal, you must finish it. You cannot abort your race somewhere in the middle; you have to cross the finish line and you have to cross it before anyone else. The key is to be committed to your own self, keep your promises and say what you're going to do while doing what you said you were going to do.

Once you have started, you must finish. This is really important. You do not have to wait for the perfect moment in fact when you finish what you start you gain a sense of accomplishment and with that comes more confidence. You do not have to continue postponing until a "better" time comes. If you want to start a bit early, start early. If you think you need to work a bit late, work a bit late. If you think you should make your time for something important, make time for it.

The point is, do whatever it takes to get the job done. It is all about keeping promises and being true to your own self. When you adopt this core principle in your heart, you will feel an internal pressure, motivating you to do whatever you need to do. When I make a vow to myself to complete a particular task and fail to do it, I get furious with myself. I think of how I should have and could have gotten it done. I experience guilt. This guilt, this anger and this restlessness actually works in my favor. You have to keep yourself, your willingness, your dedication and your commitment at the top, and you have to keep your own priorities set high. You must realize that it is all about your actions; nobody else will do it for you. As I said earlier, if it's meant to be, it's up to me.

As we discuss great work ethic is important to note that this does not mean that in keeping yourself and your goals before everything, you stomp all over your competitors and those around you working in a similar capacity or in the same environment. Great work ethic is not all about dedication, commitment, success and getting things done. It is also about empathy and compassion and human values. If you are a leader or are working in an upper managerial capacity, this becomes even more important. You cannot be a tyrant or a dictator. You cannot simply issue commands and have them be obeyed. You must listen. You must be open to views and opinions. You must keep an eye for everyone's betterment. And you must ensure that everyone around you also makes it to the finish line.

Motivate them, inspire them and talk to them about your own approach. Become their beacon of guidance and inspiration and you will see it infuse positive outcomes into your goals and your journey too. When you teach something, you learn it twice, and learning twice means that you are set for improving and developing your signature standard operating procedures.

In my work life, I do not necessarily prefer to have the last word because I know there is always room for improvement. I do not consider myself a know-it-all. I believe that dedication, commitment and hard works gets things done but it is empathy, compassion and humility that make one great. Relationships and networking are important in professional life. You cannot make it alone. You need people alongside you on the journey. You've likely heard the statement "Iron sharpens iron."

Now that we understand how a great work ethic helps elevate you on the ladder of success, you need to evolve your own set of professional values and your own work procedures. You need to evolve your signature procedures and plan of action. You cannot stop midway through your journey and lose hope. You must keep going. Even if your pace decelerates or you are stopped at un unusual turn you may stop but do not make that stop permanent. Start again, test and learn and keep on trying. But never, ever stop.

Even with processes and procedures in hand, things will occasionally happen in an undesired way. You will aim for one thing and be redirected to something else. You will head in one direction and be made to take a U-turn. Actual scenarios will not turn out to be the way you planned.

Therefore, you must be open and flexible in all situations and your plan and course of action should be such that you can easily mold and alter them as per the reality and demand of the time and case. The ability to adapt to changing winds and adjust your sails accordingly is the quality of a great captain. Similarly, this is the measure of excellence in a good leader or manager who can instantly and skillfully modify the plan to fit the reality of the situation.

A great work ethic helps you in multiple ways. Apart from the obvious advantage they expedite you on the journey to success, they add onto your presence in your professional domain. People notice the way each of us works. If your work procedures are efficient and smart, others will want to associate with you, do business with you and join you in some ventures because they sense that you are sure to work hard, sure to work smart, and feel the energy of strong work ethic.

I remember when I worked as a salesman, I met a lady in a sales meeting. After we finished discussing the plan, offer and deal, she stopped and said, "You shouldn't be doing what you are doing." I asked what she meant by that, and her reply made my day. She said, "I am not being rude or anything, don't get me wrong. I am just impressed with your professionalism, how you communicate, the strong energy and work ethic that you carry and how you do things. You are made to work on higher managerial levels, and I believe it wouldn't take you long to reach up there."

I like this quote from Grant Cardone, "Show up early, treat people with respect and perform at the highest level till the world can't deny you!

This is truly the way it works. Your energy your work ethic, your action and your extra aura, speaks more about you, then the way in which you introduce yourself. And when it comes to your career and profession, a strong personality, effervescent energy and great attitude comes from sound work ethic. Once you have developed your work ethic, you can be sure that you are finally heading fast toward consistent growth and excellence.

6

DESIRE – SELF-AWARENESS
AND SPIRITUAL
AWAKENING

"The light you are looking for has always been within."

"In order to succeed, your desire for success should be greater than your fear of failure."

I n short, desire is the seed out of which success is born.

But what is desire actually?

By definition, desire is a strong feeling to want something, to have something, or to wish for something to happen. It is not eagerness or anticipation or anything so shallow. It is, rather, a deep enlightenment that slowly rises and invokes an intense feeling from within, making you want to pursue something with all your heart.

The way I look at it is, everybody has his own desire within himself, in a deep slumber, that needs to be awakened. That desire could be anything or may relate to any area of one's life, be it family, education or profession. You might have a desire to have a family. Perhaps you want to own your own business or maybe you want to succeed in your career.

In my case, I desired to move up the ladder in my professional sales environment. I desired to have everything I wished for during my days of struggle. I desired to be so successful that I would actually be able to pay it back and contribute toward a positive change in the world. I always had a desire to succeed and get to a point where I was able to help others.

You can't teach someone to have desire. It has to come from within each of us. If it does not come from within, it can be a wish or a hope or a want, but it isn't desire. Before it comes from within, however, you have to believe and rest assured that the desire is and has always been within you, waiting for the perfect time to rise and shake you up. When it does, it will be as though you awoke from a dream and realized that this is what you were made to do. The spark is always there, but you have to light it up. All of a sudden, it will click, make its presence felt, and you will feel a surge of joy, excitement, fear and anxiousness all at once. You will feel fueled up and charged to set yourself toward the pursuit of your desire.

Desire isn't one of those things that needs to be there in order to make something happen, but when you have desire, your movement toward whatever your trying to accomplish is so much more powerful that it quickens or surges, and paves the way for accomplishment, making miracles happen, turning impossible into possible. It was desire that made man reach the moon, invade far-off lands and oceans and reach out into the expanse of the galaxies to look for traces of life beyond. Desires are crazy, and they make crazy ideas into reality.

The good news is that desire helps make things happen. The bad news is that you can't teach or preach or adopt or learn to have desire. It must come from within. But how do we know that we have a purpose or desire burning within?

In the previous chapters I discussed student mentality, consistent learning, and the importance of constantly adding to and improving our knowledge. People generally perceive desire as something unattainable, something that is super-natural and beyond human reach. They also say that a desire for money or prosperity or worldly riches is not actually a desire, but a materialistic want. I find that quite funny, for I believe that people have their own desires that they aspire to achieve. They could be anything aesthetic, abstract or materialistic. There is nothing wrong with any approach, but I believe that when you talk about professional success and career growth, you cannot talk about success without talking about money.

When you say you want to succeed, a discussion about money is required. The world we live no longer belongs to the ice age when people lived in caves and hunted for food. Today, the cost of life and living is getting pricier by the day. In the professional realm, the concept of success without money or riches sounds bland. Your skills and experience and awards and qualifications may have their value and worth, but your success will only be measured by how profitably you have cashed in on your strengths.

It is interesting to hear people say things such as, "You can't chase money, and if your goals remain confined to making money, you will fall flat on your face." The reality is, in order to survive in this world, money has to be made.

Not all desires are worth your time and effort, however. Your mind will continue to generate ideas and desires and might even cause you to go mad over them. The point is to flourish and pay heed to desires that will turn out to be your stepping stones to success. There will be desires that will only drain you of energy and won't pay you back. If you want to achieve success and prosperity in life, it is important that you pursue desires that will help you along your journey.

How do you determine which desires will help you climb the ladder of success? The answer is that, this, too, just like the desire itself, must come from within. This happens when you start realizing what is in it for you. There's a famous saying: "Do what you love; the money will follow." There's also another saying: "You must be willing to do the things today that others won't do in order to have the things tomorrow others won't have." In the case of someone who wants to be incredibly successful to be able to give back, earning money is a key component of that desire. Focus first on yourself so that you can help others. It is critically important to know what it is that you are going for.

If you have a clear purpose, you will think beyond the point when you have actually achieved it. For example, I am still not at that point where I can buy my mom a house with cash, and another of my visions or goals is as big as creating a charity to assist those who are struggling financially.

When you have a desire to accomplish something, and then you actually accomplish it, then you can give back. It is not and it should not be that you are suddenly superior or extraordinary; instead, it is and it should be that you become a metaphor for accomplishment. You show that success is possible and that there is possibility for everyone.

Awareness is knowledge or perception of a situation or fact. As you grow and experience life, you become more and more aware. It ties in with the concept of student mentality. Awareness and, specifically, self-awareness allows your sub-conscious mind to be optimistic. I mentioned a quote from Buddha in the previous chapter: "What you think you eventually become." So, when you are continuously trying to succeed and putting positive images in your mind, your sub-conscious will reciprocate. I remember learning about making a vision board and that if you believe, you will achieve because the vision stands right in front of you. So I did just that. I created a vision board for myself in my days of struggle, and I'd think about ways to acquire the things I have now. When you really want something, you have to go and get it. When you dream and you know what is the calling of your soul, you start living the dream. You realize that things are aligning themselves in perfect unison. Your routines, thought processes and actions begin to revolve around that dream. It can make you restless. It can keep you awake, and it can show up in your nighttime dreams. It is at that point when you know that this is what you're made for; this is the purpose of your life.

Desires vary from person to person. I spent my early life deprived of and struggling for life's basic necessities, so my desire at that time was to achieve what many had achieved. For people who never had it this tough, their desires may be different. My point is, we all have desires, but it is not necessary that we both know and realize them simultaneously. It is a matter of the right time and situation before the awareness and realization dawn together, igniting the spark that has always been within, turning it into a vibrant flame. The universe can conspire to help you achieve, but it will only happen when you are truly ready to do so.

Self-awareness is key. If you are not aware of your actual reality, you will not know what you truly want out of life and what is that you are truly pursing. Wandering through the labyrinth of oblivion, you will likely begin to question your existence.

However, self-awareness itself won't automatically shower your life with a pleasant, jubilant feeling or a pure ecstasy. It is more that it allows you to shed all the veils that you have so cleverly put on in an attempt to hide your reality not from the world, but sometimes from your own self.

You will feel alone in a deep solitude, and you'll stand in front of a mirror that is all set to show you who you actually are. And then, looking straight into your own eyes, you will begin to remove all the masks that you have put on, one after another, for your entire life, mistaking them for your actual identity. When you shed off everything between your perceived and actual reality, the truest version of yourself will look back at you, and it could be someone so unfamiliar that you might realize you've never known him at all.

Remember that reality will never come to you in a beautifully wrapped present. It will reveal itself when you least expect it.

This moment is the most crucial of your life's journey. You might run away, as do most people who end up losing the race. Or, you might choose to accept it to its core, embrace yourself and all your strengths and weakness, angles and demons, bright and dark sides. It is only when you do this that you realize what you should improve and, what you need to learn in order to become the best version of yourself. When you do this, you will realize that everything begins to fall into place. With regard to tasks you were constantly failing at, you will realize where you were lagging behind, and you will know with what you need to armor yourself to ace it like a boss.

If you, like many others, are struggling to make it through the spiral of challenges, know that you are not alone. We must all bear our own fair share of blessings and struggles, and everyone is busy fighting his own personal battles.

Whatever your circumstances may be, rest assured that the harder it is for you, the more sustained your success will be. The key is to keep yourself in the process of self-discovery, know your passion, overcome your weakness and improve your core strengths. And how do we keep ourselves motivated for this? By counting our blessings and acknowledging that we have much to be grateful for. Because you have so much to be thankful for, it comes with bigger obligation to share a bit of it with those who do not have it and those who are not as privileged.

The universe operates on the principle of give and take. The more you give, the more you will gain. The more you gain, the more you can contribute. And apparently, the more you take things for granted, the less you will be blessed with. The universe maintains itself in a perfect state of equilibrium through this principle.

As Rumi said, "What you seek is seeking you."

Tying all thoughts together, self-realization gives you a strong power and authority over yourself. This power can be constructive and positive or destructive and negative. If you hold it close to your heart, make a consistent effort and don't lose your motivation, the desire and the self-realization will take you toward self-actualization.

I believe that you alone are responsible for what you do with your life. I have always seen my life as my sole responsibility, with me being the only one accountable for myself. Even when accidents have happened, I thought I might have done something negative along the way that came back to me. Don't get me wrong; God has your back. God has blessed you to be you, and He's blessed your choices and your decisions if they are with good intent. Therefore, you earn good things too. There are no such things as miracles or coincidence. It's God. All that you do, good or bad, will come back to you. And all that comes back to you, you earned along the way.

As I reflect on my days of struggle, my deprived childhood where we had to long for even life's basic necessities, I remember how I felt when I saw kids my age, flaunting their shoes and clothes and toys and everything that almost everyone else seemed to have

I could have made that my weakness; I could have lost my self-eteem and self-belief, considering myself inferior to all others. I could have started believing myself unworthy of all this.

But, I didn't!

Rather, I took it as a challenge.

I constantly reminded myself that I did not like this phase of my life at all, and I would not ensure that it didn't stretch over my entire life.

I struggled. I persisted. I kept my hopes and beliefs high. And I persevered through the thick and thin. The funny thing is, you will have many wins and some losses along the way, but growth is never over till you literally die. I believe you can continue to learn about life and yourself every day.

The journey is not always nice or pretty. It is not always smooth or clear. But if you have the flame of desire and the armor of your strengths, you are good to go and can take on any challenge of your life.

"If something burns your soul with purpose and desire, it's your duty to be reduced to ashes by it. Any other form of existence will be yet another dull book in the library of life."

—Charles Bukowski

7

TIME

When you are heading toward your goal, pursuing your desires and battling the challenges life throws at you along the way, it often happens that the goal, the destiny, the dream and the vision all of a sudden lose their charm.

A million questions begin popping up in our minds; the destiny seems so far off, beyond your reach. We start thinking that maybe our goals and visions are unrealistic. We start thinking that maybe we have aspired for something that is so not accessible, something that is impractical and, perhaps, even impossible. We might even start feeling like blindfolded fools that have been running with no sense of direction.

Negative thoughts like these are normal, especially when you are in pursuit of something great and worthwhile. What is not acceptable is allowing this pessimism to take over. Of course we have our own limits of patience and tolerance, but it is in the greatest of pursuits that we are tested the hardest.

It is times like these that determine whether you will be a loser or a champion. If, in such times, you manage to survive, keep your cool and stand steadfast on the belief that, once you get a hold of things, your journey will be smooth and that, sooner or later, you will make it to your ultimate goal. Congratulations, for you are already past the negative phase.

Time has the potential to grow, pessimism can create illusions about your ideals of success and prosperity. You may never know exactly how much time it will take for you to cross the finish line. This ambiguity in the area of time begins to invoke an uncertainty when it comes to your goal. It can begin to make them feel like a far-fetched fantasy. What you need most at this phase of your journey is consistency, belief and perseverance.

Consistency is considered the habit of winners. It is the very measure of how far you will go and where you will land.

Consistency and persistency are everyday habits. Their purpose is to maintain a uniform level of motivation and efforts every-day until your dream is achieved. The challenge is managing to get through those days when you are low on energy and motivation and nothing excites you but you still wake up and put in the effort because you know it is consistency and persistency that will take you forward. The only other way is to stop and give up, and this isn't a choice you will make if you are determined to succeed. Consistency and persistency are the promises you make to yourself.

As Tony Robbins said, "It is not what we do every once in a while that shapes our live. It is what we do consistently."

If you wish to be a better version of yourself, you need consistent improvement.

If you want to seek a dream qualification, you need consistent study.

If you want to be promoted or be more successful, you need consistent, persistent input of effort.

Consistency demands that you progress through the entire journey with the same zeal and zest. Consistency combined with persistency means that you escalate your magnitude of effort and motivation as you proceed rather than gradually losing momentum in both areas. As Steve Jobs said, "I am convinced that about half of what separates the successful entrepreneurs from the non-successful ones is pure perseverance."

Remember that you always have a choice. You can either choose to be consistent or choose to give up. It is the choice that determines your fate. Giving up is always the easiest way out. Giving up is the ultimate and abrupt halt to all your efforts and struggles. But remember, "Winners never quit and quitters never win." Now I don't want someone to take this out of context either. Having said that, in a case where you need to leave or quit a place of employment for the betterment of your own happiness or because you're moving on to further opportunities, that does not mean your quitting.

In my experience, this is the most concise explanation of the phenomenon of success. I believe it is the choice between perseverance and giving up that denotes the fine demarcation between the paths of losers and winners. Persistence demands stamina, resilience and guts, and not everyone has it at first, it is over time that you can begin to build that muscle.

It is the most courageous of hearts, the strongest of minds and the craziest of rebels who challenge the status quo of their own lives and break through their limitations. Who opts for the path of consistency and struggle that others fear treading. It is those who choose to persist and keep up with the effort and struggle who make it to the top, pass the competitors and a chanting, clapping crowd, eventually making it to the stage to lift their trophy.

Consistency does not mean, however, that you keep on doing the same things for years, hoping to ultimately reach your goals. This also could be taken out of context because the definition of insanity is doing the same thing over and over while expecting different results. Consistency means that you keep your morale high while increasing your efforts and never lose hope in the process. If you manage to sustain the same pace for years, you will stay at the same place and position for your entire life. If you want to excel, you must be consistent while increasing your efforts.

If you continue being a part of the system--the regular, ordinary scheme of operations--waking up in the morning, going to school, returning home and following the same programmed routine, you will become ordinary and just another within the population. The concept of success is born a step ahead of where normalcy and the regular scheme of things end. Success is born during the extra mile, when you've gone above and beyond.

Remember that success in its entirety is a two-way process. You can do more when you have more. And when you have more, you can do more. The essential crux of success is based on the Law of Attraction. As love begets love, hate begets hate, fears beget fears and constraints beget constraints, success and prosperity likewise pull in more of their kind. The point is that when you do the right things the right things start happening in your life. Similarly, when you do bad, bad things happen in return.

Through my entire journey of struggle, I knew and believed right from the start that all I had to be concerned about was making sure that I gave it my best, put in optimum efforts and utilized my talents, skills and strengths in the best way possible.

I believe that when you give your best, something better than your best comes back to you. It is your reward, your achievement and your success. And that is how it worked for me. In this world where everything from food to shopping to communication is available in an instant, success still cannot be cooked overnight.

You're not going to go to sleep broke one night and wake up a millionaire the very next day unless you win a lottery. And even if you win a lottery, you might become a millionaire, but you won't be seen as successful in the truest sense of the word. In fact, many lose the money.

I believe that true success goes beyond riches and wealth, meaning success goes beyond materialistic gains. It is a sense of accomplishment when getting the job gets done. Your mental solace. A clear voice saying inside that you made it. That whatever you have been through was worth it. It lifts your head up, fills you with a revitalizing energy that turns out to be a clear reassurance that you have reached your goal and, the horizon is all yours. You can go wherever you want and, you can achieve whatever you wish for.

However, it only happens when you have devoted yourself to your own reasons why, your cause, your own dream and your ultimate life goal. When you have consumed everything that you have and you have nothing more to lose. When you pass one milestone, then another and then another. In this quest to going the extra mile, you get so far ahead that there is no going back to that place of poverty. When you have burned all bridges and set your boats on fire, you will know that and the only way to make it to the other side of the ocean of struggles is to swim. I noted this quote by Charles Bukowski earlier: "If something burns your soul with purpose and desire, it's your duty to be reduced to ashes by it. Any other form of existence will be yet another dull book in the library of life."

Success, in its truest sense, is a matter of time, coupled with consistent efforts. When it is time, it is time. Nobody can change that or snatch that away from you. You do have a degree of control and authority over time. You can force time to change in your favor, and you can summon success earlier than it may be pre-destined to occur.

Your efforts and your right to choose your path are in your hands. It is only a matter of your own choice. If you decide to put in your best put in your best. Do it while defying all odds. Do it beyond the constraints of fate and destiny, and rest assured that sooner or later, your time will come. As Paulo Coelho said, "When you want something with all your heart, all the universe conspires to help you achieve it."

Everyone goes through a time in life when nothing makes sense. No matter how much you try to solve the riddle of your life, you never seem to find the last puzzle piece to complete the picture. Everything seems vague. The future seems distant. Lurking in the labyrinth of oblivion, you start questioning your existence. Negativity surrounds you, and there seems no way past the gloom. It seems as if you will have to suffer for your entire life.

And then, all of a sudden, realization dawns upon you, pieces start falling into place. The clouds of despair begin moving away to reveal the silver lining and a vibrant rainbow of hope and happiness. Sunshine takes over your world and starts nurturing your dreams. Everything that seemed as distant as the stars comes well within your reach. Everything that seemed impossible to achieve is enclosed within your hands.

We will all experience this at some point in life. I made it through, and so will you. Whatever stage of life you are struggling with, be it the early childhood days or school or your career ladder, things will work out. It can sometimes feel like a vicious cycle, but you simply have to be patient. You have to persist, and you must not give up. I started small, by getting just a job to get by. My Ground Zero was way below that of the average person.

But with the clear vision to create a guiding beacon, and with a sense of purpose in heart, I crawled and I stumbled, but I never stopped. I kept on going through the tunnel of struggles., I managed to make peace with my weaknesses and improve myself along the way. I overcame my fears. I survived when life tried to choke me to death.

While many people wish not to land in a corporate set-up until the start of their career, I started early at the age of 13 mowing people's lawns. There was no other way; those were the cards that were dealt to me. I didn't like it; I never liked my poverty. I didn't necessarily like the way we used to live. But rather than drown in the spiral of disparity and unfavorable circumstances, I pushed through and persevered. I constructed a temple of hope inside my heart.

Some might call it a miracle, some might call it fate, some might say it was destiny. I believe it was the result of a great attitude, hard work, student mentality, confidence, persistency, consistency and time. The whole idea, therefore, is to focus on what is within your control in these areas. You have to persevere until what it is you're going after comes to fruition, and soon, you will see your time arrive. As I often like to say: "Remember, stay committed, stay focused…. Be the light!"